R394.268
A546k

DETROIT PUBLIC LIBRARY

W9-CAE-857

DETROIT PUBLIC LIBRARY

CHANEY BRANCH LIBRARY
16101 W. GRAND RIVER
DETROIT, MI 48227

DATE DUE

BC-3

KWANZAA
An Everyday Resource and Instructional Guide

David A. Anderson/SANKOFA

DETROIT
PUBLIC
LIBRARY

GUMBS & THOMAS Publishers, Inc.
New York

Anderson, David A.
    Kwanzaa an everyday resource and instructional guide / David A.
Anderson.
    p. cm.
    Includes bibliographical references and index.
    ISBN 0-936073-15-2

    1. Kwanzaa. 2. Afro-Americans--Social life and customs--Study and
teaching. 3. Harvest festivals--United States--Study and teaching.
I. Title.

GT4403.A5 1992   394.268
                                        QBI91-1714

Design: Bob Gumbs and Ademola Olugebefola

Symbols of Adinkra Cloth on pages IV, VIII, 9, 25, 44, 46, 48, 54, 58, 60, reference: Dr. Kwaku Ofori Ansah

Copyright © 1992 by David A. Anderson and Gumbs & Thomas Publishers, Inc.

All rights reserved. No part of this publication may be reproduced or transmitted in any form or by any means, electronic
or mechanical, including photocopy, recording or any information storage and retrieval system, without permission in
writing from the publishers.

ISBN: 0936073-15-2

Photo credit: D. McKinney Anderson

David A. Anderson

David A. Anderson has many years of professional experience in teaching, administration, community organization and assisting adult learners pursue careers in human service fields. He has taught at Rochester Institute of Technology, University of Rochester School of Medicine and Dentistry, Colgate Divinity School and The State University of New York Brockport.

Mr. Anderson has a BFA in Photography, from Rochester Institute of Technology, an MA in Education from Syracuse University and a Ph.D., in Education Administration, from the Union Institute of Cincinnati.

David is also a performing storyteller. He draws upon the folklore of traditional African and African American culture to promote cross cultural appreciation. As a traditional Griot, he has been featured in major Festivals throughout the United States and he has had storytelling residencies in Columbus, Ohio; Great Valley, and Buffalo, New York; Columbia, Maryland; Waukegan, Illinois and Georgetown, South Carolina.

Dr. Anderson began telling stories publicly in 1981 as part of the healing process called for by the death of his father. Storytelling has enhanced "The Cultural Heritage of African-American Children," a course he developed and teaches for the State University of New York, at Brockport. Similarly, storytelling is essential to this work in Parent Education for the Rochester City School District, and as a convenor of Rochester's annual Kwanzaa celebration.

III

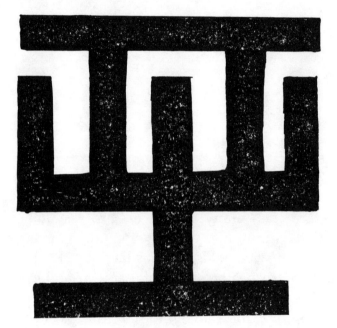

HWEMUDUA
(Searching rod or measuring rod)
Symbol of Excellence, Quality,
Perfection and Knowledge.

IV

Contents

PREFACE   1

Chapter 1 (moja)

Introduction to Kwanzaa   5
  • Preparation and Implementation   7

Chapter 2 (mbili)

A Kwanzaa Theme Unit for Children   11
  • Description   11

  • Objectives   11

  • Preparation   12

  • Strategies:

      1. Parents planning a community-based karamu   12
      2. Introduce the concept of holiday...   12
      3. Ask students...what they have learned from parents...   13
      4. Review the Seven Principles (Nguzo Saba)   14
      5. How to practice Nguzo Saba   15
      6. Students interpret Nguzo Saba   16
      7. Kiswahili: Introducing the language...   17
      8. What gives a thing its value?   20
      9. Examine quilt making as...development of stories   21
     10. Connect valuing, wisdom and self-determination   22

Chapter 3 (tanu)

The Harvest Concept in the Kwanzaa Holiday: 27
A Theme Unit for Youths
  • Description   27

  • Objectives   28

  • Strategies: 28

1. Introduce the concept of holiday...   28
2. Search for the concept of harvest   29
3. Display the Kwanzaa ritual symbols   30
4. Diversity among the peoples of Africa...   31
5. Greet students with, "Habari gani" ("What's the news")   31
6. Discuss separation from family in historical and trans-
   Atlantic contexts   32
7. Develop process for "gathering-in" (Karamu)   33
8. Fine tune and rehearse Karamu plan   34
9. Plan a student-led assembly as tune-up for Karamu   35
10. Autobiography as illustration of values inherent in Kwanzaa   38
11. Explore values as resources for overcoming adversity   38
12. Implementing Karamu   41
13. Evaluation Project   42
14. Sample content and format for report-l   43

AFTERWORD   45
More Words   47

APPENDIX   49
Materials Used or Consulted   51
Free and Cued Retelling   53
Karamu Planning Outline   54
How To Practice Nguzo Saba - A Photo Essay   56

INDEX   59

SANKOFA
(Go back to fetch it)
Symbol of the Wisdom in Learning
From The Past in Building the Future.

Preface

About eight years ago Delta Nu Omega chapter of Alpha Kappa Alpha Sorority, invited me to conduct a Kwanzaa workshop for their families and friends. Similarly, I have aided the Perinton, New York African American Heritage Committee in its annual "gathering-in" of member families. Also, I have acted as convenor of the Rochester Kwanzaa Committee in its planning and implementing of that city's annual Kwanzaa celebration.

A majority of the sorors and many in the Perinton group are both teachers and mothers. They carry their investment in Kwanzaa into both roles and thus have provided opportunities for me to bring what I am learning about Kwanzaa into classrooms and other institutions. These parents and teachers can describe the respectful relationships shared by the teachers that taught them and the parents that raised them. They confess that such foundations were instrumental in preparing them for confrontations with systems and individuals that would try to degrade them.

That such imagery issues from earlier times and was nurtured in more unified African American communities only heightens the need to awaken children to the African American cultural heritage. Kwanzaa is a resource that addresses the self-esteem issue comprehensively: one is called to celebrate current efforts as well as past glories; preparation for the future as well as triumph over yesterday's injustices.

Chapter One of *Kwanzaa: An Everyday Resource and Instructional Guide* is a general review of what Kwanzaa is and is not, plus a description of procedures, 1 materials and structure. Chapters Two and Three provide interdisciplinary theme units - one for children under age 13 and one for older youths. Both units emphasize the seven principles undergirding Kwanzaa, and provide a variety of activities that can help people learn these principles.

A number of very fine trade books are incorporated into the strategies and activities that form the core of this guide. Appendix (   ), "Materials Used or Consulted," lists books as well as recordings and other audiovisuals. Each is in print as of September 15, 1991, and the books are relatively inexpensive. Each family should own several, both for reference and for the pleasure to be found in good children's literature. Parents should consider purchasing the storybooks and recordings for zawadi, i.e., Kwanzaa gifts. My personal favorites are marked by asterisk(*) in "Materials Used or Consulted."

Although Chapter Three is directed to the teacher of older youths, other teachers will benefit from reading it, especially the activities described under "Develop a Process for Gathering-In". Teachers at both levels are strongly urged to facilitate their students' planning and implementation of the "in-gathering", i.e., the Karamu or culminating event.

The activities that inform this journey into Kwanzaa are presented in sufficient detail to function as a how-to manual. Yet the intent is to provide guidance, not prescription. Adults committed to the development of children and youths are necessarily creative. Those able to see that African Americans are linked to a viable culture will use this book to extend their own and their students' appreciation of African American culture.

To Delta Nu Omega Chapter of Alpha Kappa Alpha Sorority for opening the door and maintaining confidence in me; to the Perinton African American Heritage Committee; to colleagues in the Rochester Kwanzaa Committee, and the dozen or more Rochester City School District teachers who early on checked it out and keep on running it down to the children; to my wife Ruth, who not only builds Kwanzaa into the instruction she provides for middle school students, but accepts as a fact of life that our December 26 wedding anniversary will usually be spent trying to help folks new to Kwanzaa get into it; to all, asante sana.

David A. Anderson/SANKOFA

Illustration by Chris Hall from *Let's Celebrate Kwanzaa* by Helen Davis Thompson - Gumbs & Thomas Publishers, New York.

Introduction to Kwanzaa

What is Kwanzaa?

Kwanzaa is affirmation - a way of saying, "Yes, African American people are people of history, of the present and of the future. Kwanzaa is motivation to African American people to "keep on keeping on."

Kwanzaa is a process way of guiding African American learners to high performance and achievement standards. It is a curriculum for helping Euro-American learners, Asian American learners - learners of every cultural background to see African Americans as people with assets and deficits, achievements and failures - a people sometimes crying "The Weary Blues," [1] yet singing "a song full of the hope that the present has brought us." [2]

Kwanzaa was created in the 1960s to help guide the energies African Americans were hurling against the forces of racial oppression. It called for serious study of the unique and richly human struggle that was at the core of African American culture. The core is still intact, enriched by the experiences of the newest generation of Americans. African Americans function among people of diverse backgrounds and interests. Thus Kwanzaa is also a school curriculum for learners that make up that diversity.

---

[1] A poem by Langston Hughes, published 1926.
[2] A poem by James Weldon Johnson, set to music by his brother, J. Rosamond Johnson, and popularly known as the "Black National Anthem."

Who is this Guide for?

KWANZAA: An Everyday Resource and Instructional Guide, is designed for parents and teachers — individual teachers and entire faculties — who entertain the idea that African American students are more than the sum of the white-black gap in achievement scores and suspension rates. Whether you teach out of parental love and duty; whether you teach in public or parochial school, day care center, prison, public library, museum, or religious education program, the activities in this book can:

Enrich the content and substance of your teaching;

Enhance your students' understanding of African American culture; and

Enhance your students' appreciation of the diversity of the American cultural mix.

This teacher's guide will help you understand that KWANZAA is not:

A substitute for Christmas

An imitation Chanukah

The Six o'clock News report of another drug-related slaying about them folks they call "minorities".

Words and Deeds: The Community Interprets Kwanzaa

Each day of Kwanzaa is devoted to a specific principle. But each principle calls forth deeper social, spiritual and moral commitment. These seven principles, called NGUZO SABA, provide the philosophical foundation of Kwanzaa. These are but words until people begin to live them. KWANZAA IS:

Delores and George making two sweet, sweet babies and she giving birth to the center of African American culture, too. (UMOJA: Unity)

Young "Cecil talkin' 'bout makin' a film to tell the chil'ren that drugs is a robber and a thief; and then him doin' it, too." (KUJICHAGULIA: Self Determination)

Miss Rosa Weems organizing a bunch of volunteers to feed folks in the neighborhood - no questions asked. (UJIMA: Collective Work and Responsibility)

Terry and Chaka making books about and by African Americans good business (they call it Kitabu Kingdom) for and in the community. (UJAMAA: Cooperative Economics)

Bruce raising his daughter by himself, and helping 15 "single-parent" mothers keep their boys and girls on the right track. (NIA: Purpose)

Gladys - "She the only one of us a teacher out there at the white school; but she be doin' stuff with the chil'ren to let 'em know the Black peoples be worth a lots." (KUUMBA: Creativity)

"...the quilt Big Mama left us. It's got a patch that come from Willie Roy's overalls. May Jane's bedspread is in there, too. There's lots more of us in there, too. Oh, it's got some of our history sewed up in it...I'm saving Big Mama's quilt for you - for when you be ready to have your first baby." (IMANI: Faith)

CELEBRATION

Kwanzaa is an African American celebration observed during the seven-day period from December 26 through January 1. Created in 1966 by Dr. Maulana Ron Karenga, Kwanzaa is based on traditional harvest festivals traditionally practiced throughout Africa. Kwanzaa brings families and communities together to celebrate the "fruits" of their year's labors, to give thanks (asante), to evaluate their achievements and contributions to the family and community and to lay plans and set goals for the year ahead.

As with all celebrations, there are symbols associated with Kwanzaa that reinforce the principles:

MKEKA (M-kay-cah)	A straw mat - this represents the foundation upon which All other tradtions rest.
KINARA (Kee-nah-rah)	A seven place candle holder. This represents the original stalk, ancestry or genealogy from which we have sprung; i.e., the African beginnings.
MISHUMAA SABA (Mee-shoo-maah sah-bah)	Seven candles - three red; three green; one black - represent each of the seven principles.
MUHINDI (Moo-heen-dee)	Ears of corn - one for each child in the family, representing the product, or the offspring of the stalk or the parents, and all the challenges and hopes children bring.
MAZAO (Mah-zah-oh)	Crops (fruits, nuts, vegetables) - results or fruits of the harvest: i.e., collective, productive effort.
ZAWADI (Sah-wah-dee)	Gifts. On the last day of Kwanzaa, meaningful gifts, particularly for children, should encourage growth and self-development during the coming year.
KIKOMBE CHA UMOJA (Kee-coam-bay chah-oo-moe-jah)	The unity cup - a special vessel used exclusively in performing of libation ritual.

Preparation and Implementation

All of the symbols, including the ZAWADI, and fresh fruits and nuts, are placed on the mkeka. Families gather each day to light the appropriate mishumaa: black on December 26; black and red on December 27; black, red and green on December 28, etc.

Following the candle-lighting, the family discusses the principle of the day, how it relates to their lives, individually, as a family and as a community. A moment of silence might be observed, libation poured to the ancestors, an improvised prayer said, poems or thoughts shared, songs sung, etc. Greetings during Kwanzaa take the form of a question, "HABARI GANI?" (What is the news?). The response is the principle of the day (ex: "UMOJA," for the first day, unity).

Related Activities

Fasting from dawn to dusk is an option practiced by some adults. After sundown only fruits, nuts, vegetables and juices are consumed. Fasting represents a cleansing of the body as we cleanse our minds and spirits for the coming year.

The *KARAMU (Feast)* takes place on December 31. Maulana Karenga, the creator of the Kwanzaa celebration also encourages creativity in making the ceremony fit the family's resources and needs. The family gathers friends and neighbors for the evening to feast and make merry. Children are given gifts to be opened January 1; games are played, stories and folktales told, songs sung and people prepare to plant the seeds for a good and prosperous year ahead. In addition to the candle-lighting ceremony, the KIKOMBE CHA UMOJA (unity cup) is passed for all to share in the covenant. After sipping juice from KIKOMBE CHA UMOJA, each person says, "Harambee." After the unity cup has passed through each person's hands, all give seven rousing HARAMBEES.

Children are given an important role in Kwanzaa and are encouraged to make decorations (red, black and green), design ankhs (symbols of life) and suns (symbol of creation and growth) for display around the house. They also learn songs and games that provide reinforcement.

Red, Black and Green are the colors of Kwanzaa. Red is for the struggle for self-determination waged by the ancestors, and for the fire in our hearts which guides us to work hard for the things in which we believe. Black stands for the people, for without people there can be neither struggle nor hope. Green is for the earth that gives us life, and for our youths and the new ideas they bring (Karenga).

Kwanzaa presents schools with exceptional opportunities to strengthen alliances with students' families. It is a natural rich curriculum that can reduce the trauma attending the schooling establishment's spastic movements toward multicultural education. Each year more African American families become aware of Kwanzaa. Also, relevant practices are still being created by individual families and communities at large. Parents can initiate out of classroom Kwanzaa activities, and they must respond to teacher initiatives. By initiating, and at the same time responding to teacher initiatives, parents help their children, and their children's peers, to move beyond the events and into living the principles.

FUNTUMMIREKU DENKYEMMIREKU
(Two headed crocodile with one stomach)
Symbol of Unity In Diversity and Of Democracy.

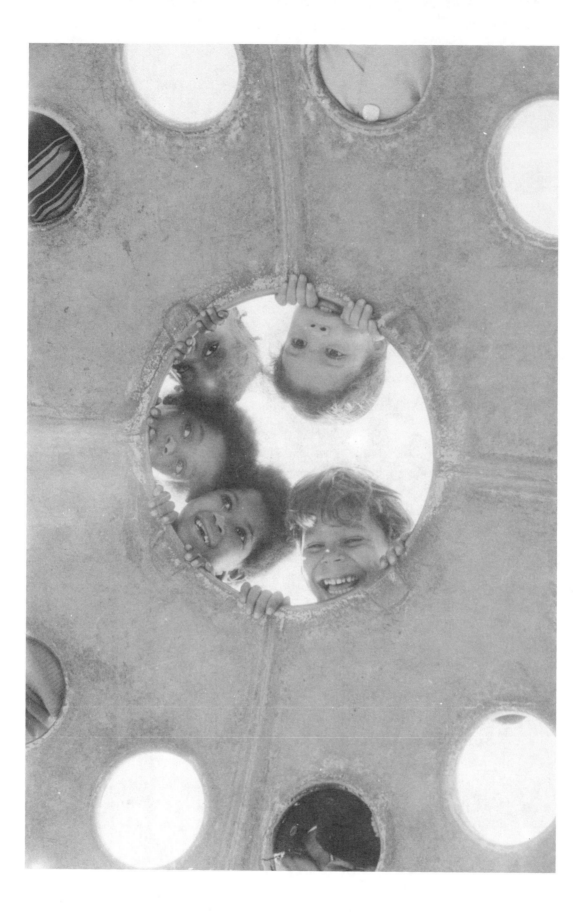

10   Children in the Round by Pat Davis courtesy Grinnell Gallery.

CHAPTER **2**
(mbili)

A Kwanzaa Theme Unit For Children

DESCRIPTION:

This literature-based theme unit includes stories that feature four families; a picture-book with commentary on 26 African cultural groups; exercises in the use of Kiswahili, the African language from which Kwanzaa terminology is derived.

You can get the unit off to a good start by recruiting a person who is conversant with Kwanzaa, and who possesses the storyteller's flair. A strong oral presentation by one who celebrates Kwanzaa establishes the holiday as something real and valued. Throughout the unit there are opportunities to involve parents.

This unit has applications in social studies, art, mathematics, science and music, as well as language arts.

OBJECTIVES:

After exposure to the material and human resources of this unit, students will:

1) decode previously unfamiliar words.
2) recognize and accurately use selected phrases in the Kiswahili language.
3) comprehend facts and details of the stories and of the picture essay.
4) assign Kwanzaa principles to the actions of story characters.
5) plan a culminating event, i.e., a Karamu.
6) write letters inviting family members to the Karamu.
7) participate in the Karamu.
8) Write report letters (including reactions to these activities) to relatives or friends in other communities, or to overseas pen pals.

11

PREPARATION:

Everything about Kwanzaa speaks to the overarching concern for the family. Kwanzaa represents another opportunity to strengthen ties between school and home. Given that the Kwanzaa unit you plan is likely to occur between late November and late December, you are well advised to initiate early contacts with parents to encourage them to discuss family genealogy, cultural holidays, treasured songs, stories and artifacts with their children. Ask them to help their children collect pennies they will need for the lesson on THE HUNDRED PENNY BOX. Moreover, each family should be asked to contribute to (an act of sharing) and participate in the Karamu, i.e., the culminating activity.

Individual parents can act as resource persons. They can demonstrate their skill at quilt-making and/or telling the stories behind quilts made or received by them; some can provide recipes for traditional foods. Another can sing a mood-setting rendition of a spiritual.

STRATEGY:

As your students work through the activities described under each strategy, they will acquire information for much of the content for Karamu. Planning begins immediately after introducing students to Kwanzaa.

Parents should get their churches, sororities, fraternities, lodges or other support groups involved in the effort to conduct a community-based Karamu between December 26 and January 1.

ACTIVITIES (to Prepare the Teacher):

• Read *Have a Happy...*, the Mildred Pitts Walter novel referenced in Chapter Three. Note that this story is at the center of the Karamu planning process for the older youths (pp. 33-37). Also examine, and tailor to your students' needs, the "Karamu Program Format" and the "Karamu Planning Outline;" both are in the Appendix.

• Depending on the scope of your Karamu (one class or school-wide), you will need to involve colleagues. They too should study the above material.

STUDENT ACTIVITIES:

• Introduce a decision-making process that includes concepts such as: brainstorming and clarifying ideas; forecasting and predicting; observing and defining; planning, implementing and evaluating. Simplified, the objective is to help children decide who is to be invited; what those who come to Karamu are to experience; the role(s) each child is to perform; when and where.

STRATEGY:

Introduce the concept of "holiday" as *one or more days when people set aside, or stop doing what they do on other days, so that they can celebrate a special event or history.*

ACTIVITIES:

• Ask for examples of holidays. Discuss each one for the purpose of getting students to distinguish between taking the day off to shop, versus engaging in practices or rituals that commemorate an event or honor a person. Use the calendars cited in the Appendix as "Material Used or Consulted" to guide discussion of ethnic and religious holidays. Contrast symbols grounded in core traditions to fads and commercial trappings. Conclude this introductory phase by announcing that:

> For the next (number of days/weeks) we will set aside some time each day to study the holiday called Kwanzaa. Kwanzaa is a time when many African Americans gather-in family and friends to honor the best of the old times and celebrate the opportunity to do better in the new times. Each of us can learn something good as we study Kwanzaa.

• Your version of the foregoing statement would be incorporated in your letter to parents, consistent with the recommendations cited above under "Preparation." Have students deliver the letters as they follow through on engaging their family members, et. al., in discussion of "holiday" and "gathering-in."

Parents initiate at-home (and in community support group) discussion of "commemorations" of significant events, e.g., December 1, 1955: Rosa Parks refuses to give up her bus seat, thereby sparking the civil rights movement: December 3, 1845 Frederick Douglass publishes the North Star, thereby sharpening the battle to end slavery.

STRATEGY:

Ask students to tell what they have learned about holidays from their parents or esteemed elders.

ACTIVITIES:

• Have students read and discuss the book, *KWANZAA*, by Deborah M. Newton Chocolate, illustrated by Melodye Rosales.

> *Synopsis:* A contemporary, urban extended family present, in story form, an explanation of the seven day holiday in which African Americans celebrate their cultural heritage. The story line is carried by an eight or nine year old child. Unlike the other characters, the child is not named, thus providing further opportunity for young readers to assume the role.

• Engage students in discussing the illustrations; help them find relationships between the child on the cover and the picture of the women and the drummers. Why is the boy (or girl) lighting candles and why is he/she dressed that way? What does the child know about the drummers and the colorfully dressed women?

• Ask students about events and celebrations for which they have dressed up. Ask about symbols and rituals or ceremonies.

• Read the story to the children. Encourage comparisons between their experiences and those depicted in the book. Help them see Kwanzaa's emphasis on happiness that results from collective *work and responsibility* - Ujima (oo-JEE-mah).

Parents recall from childhood, singing games and rhymes. Engage children in examples such as "Mary Mack, Mack, Mack," "Hambone," et. al., that can be found in SHAKE IT TO THE ONE THAT YOU LOVE THE BEST.

Shared work is team work. You help me and I help you...
If you have a problem, you can lean on me...
When I have a problem, you are able to help me. (Ujima)
        (From "How to Practice Nguzo Saba")

STRATEGY: Review the Seven Principles (Nguzo Saba)

• Bring in your resource person — that storytelling, Kwanzaa devotee — and have her/him present one or two of the principles in an engaging way. One option is the sound-filmstrip, KWANZAA: A NEW AFRO-AMERICAN HOLIDAY. Attention to the points described below will increase the value of your resource person's visit:

1. Motivate students
   a. appeal to students' interests in holidays and celebrations
   b. appeal to ethnic instincts of African American students
   c. balance the commercialism attendant to many holidays with the core values inherent in Kwanzaa
   d. discuss appreciation of cultural diversity
2. Set the Stage
   a. specify dates of celebration; overview of the tenets
   b. name, title/function, affiliations of resource person
   c. his/her expectations
   d. communicate your expectations to resource persons
   e. inform students' parents of a planned activity
   f. solicit students to introduce resource person (optional)
   g. letter of invitation written by students (optional)
   h. preparing complementary materials; securing and testing AV equipment
   i. prepare students for the presentation; prepare colleagues and their classes
3. Resource person presentation
   a. welcome and support
   b. model for students, the asking of questions
4. Student follow-up activities

5. Feedback and thank you letter to resource person

• Give examples of the five remaining principles, explaining what they are supposed to do for us and how living by such principles enhance our lives.
• Read the principles one at a time, allowing students to repeat after you. You should read them in Kiswahili and English, e.g.:

UMOJA. Umoja means unity. Unity.

• Play the recording "Seven Principles" - by Sweet Honey in the Rock
• Solicit students' interpretation of each principle. Write some of each on the chalkboard.
• Distribute copies of *Let's Celebrate Kwanzaa*, the activity book by Helen Davis Thompson. With your students, compare Thompson's definitions (pages 3,5,7,9,11,13,15) with what you write on the chalkboard.
• Encourage exploration of *Let's Celebrate Kwanzaa* and careful coloring of the illustrations.
• Play "Seven Principles" one or more times, encouraging children to sing along.

ENRICHMENT:

Secure a large vessel that can be invested with the qualities of a kikombe cha umoja (unity cup). Ask students to look for examples of people practicing Nguzo Saba - the Seven Principles. Instruct them to write the examples on a piece of tag board and put them in the kikombe cha umoja. Periodically, have students review contents of the kikombe cha umoja. Eliminate duplication. At some point make a bulletin board display, or an illustrated book of students' Nguzo Saba practices. The product should be on display before and during the Karamu. Perhaps the item you and your children choose to make can be duplicated. Each student can then have a set to facilitate family investment in the practices.

ENRICHMENT - "HOW TO PRACTICE" NGUZO SABA (En-GOO-Zoh-Sah-BAH)

Below are the slightly edited expressions of Rochester children in grades one through five. The statements were distilled from thank you letters, experience charts and other items teachers have fed back to the author.

UMOJA (oo-MOE-jah) UNITY
We can work together and play together. We must work with the people in our family and in our school and in the community of African American people.

KUJICHAGULIA (koo-jee-cha-goo-LEE-ah) SELF-DETERMINATION
It seems hard to say; but I try and try to learn it, and learn that it's about making up my mind to "keep on keeping on" in everything I do.

15

UJIMA (oo-JEE-mah) COLLECTIVE WORK AND RESPONSIBILITY
Shared work is team work. You help me and I help you...If you have a problem, you can lean on me...When I have a problem, you are able to help me.

UJAMAA (oo-JAH-mah) COOPERATIVE ECONOMICS
One person alone may not have a lot; but when each person puts in her share of work, wealth, and willpower, everybody has more.

NIA (nee-AH) PURPOSE
I want a good home, and a good school, and a good community. I will make a plan every day so I will know what to do to make the good things happen.

KUUMBA (koo-OOM-bah) CREATIVITY
I create plans for a good home and a good school and a good community...I can create beautiful things, and I will, because inside I am a beautiful person.

IMANI (ee-MAH-nee) FAITH
I believe that sharing together is good. I believe that making up my own mind and sticking to it is good too...I believe that planning and doing the right thing is good. All these things help make me beautiful inside. I believe they will help me see the beautiful old people and the little babies that will come in the future.

STRATEGY: Students Interpret Nguzo Saba

ACTIVITIES:

• Share "How to Practice Nguzo Saba" with your students. Prompt them to think about the children who made the statements (How might they be like your students?). Play the recording "Seven Principles" several times; encouraging students to "sing-a-long."

• Organize your students into cooperative learning groups. Seven is a nice number, because each group can then concentrate on reinterpreting one principle. Compile the results, do some light editing and see if the art teacher will help students turn their collective works into a dramatic poster. If the art teacher is on sabbatical, show students examples of African textiles as captured in books such as *African Textiles* (Picton and Mack) and *Shake It to the One That You Love the Best* (Mattox). Consider Adinkra stamp designs, the Asante art in which designs representing proverbs are stamped into cloth. (This is nicely explained in the January, 1985 issue of *Faces: The Magazine About People,* available from the publisher whose address is listed in the Appendix.)

• Students' design ideas are to be inscribed onto their own "How to Practice Nguzo Saba." Use an enlarging photocopier to enlarge the 8½" by 11" page of statements about 170% onto 14" x 17" sheets of paper. Leave wide enough

16

margins for students to inscribe their decorative art. Each student should complete more than one.

• Display the posters in the halls. Solicit comments from colleagues, et al. Ultimately, have your students help each other select the posters that best express each student's idea of Kwanzaa. Extra posters can be used as covers or dust jackets for the counting book project outlined under the next strategy.

STRATEGY:

Kiswahili: Introducing the language through the picture books, *Jambo Means Hello,* and *Moja Means One,* by Muriel Feelings, illustrated by Tom Feelings.

Synopsis: Together these books provide readers with some important aspects of East African life while introducing them to the Kiswahili language. There is phonetic spelling of the word concepts representing the 26 letters in the alphabet and the numbers, one through ten. Illustrator Tom Feelings enlivens each letter-word and number with a "beautifully detailed double-spread painting, ranging from the traditional greeting between elders, to a wedding scene," and "from a fireside storytelling scene to the types of clothing people wear."

ACTIVITIES:

• Greet students with "Hujambo" (oo-jahm-boe) "watoto" (wah-toe-toe), which means "Good morning, children."

• Write the words on the chalkboard, underlining each syllable as you pronounce them. Explain that you greeted them in Kiswahili, the East African language used in Kwanzaa. Enrich the discussion of this language by comparing vowel sounds in Spanish, Italian and other languages, with Kiswahili vowel sounds.

• Have students take turns reading the pages of *Umoja Means One* and *Jambo Means Hello.*

• Ask students to recite other Kiswahili words, e.g., the Seven Principles. Point out that *kwanza* (ending in single 'a') — a word meaning "first" — is different from the *Kwanzaa* (count the letters in this double vowel ending), the title of the seven-day holiday.

• Play Ella Jenkins's recording of "Jambo Means Hello."

• Distribute copies of Nguzo Saba (Seven Principles) set to a rhythm running in *my* head. It is presented here with the barest of notation, thus emphasizing that other rhythms, other words, are possible. Challenge your young rappers to beat that.

Oo-MOE-juh! Oo-MOE-juh!	UMOJA
Talkin' 'bout Unity!	
Unity!Unity!	
Koo---jee-chah-goo-L-EE-E-ah	KUJICHAGULIA
Koo---jee-chah-goo-L-EE-E-ah	

Koo---jee-chah-goo-L-EE-E-ah
---------Self! de-term-in-nation
---------Self! de-term-in-nation

Oo-JEE-mah! Oo-JEE-mah!   UJIMA
Collective work--------------
         -------Responsi-bi-i-i-lity!
Collective work--------------
         -------Responsi-bi-i-i-lity!

Oo-JAH-mah, Oo-JAH-mah   UJAMAA
Oo-JAH-mah, Oo-JAH-mah
-------Economics. Economics.
-------Economics. Economics.
Talkin' bout Cooperative----
----------Economics-------------
Cooperative--------
----------Economics

Nee-AH ----   NIA
Serious purpose ---
-----get down!
Nee-AH ----
Serious purpose ---
-----get down!

Koom-BAH, Koom-BAH   KUUMBA
Koom-BAH, Koom-BAH
--- clean up!
--- clean up!
Koom-BAH, Koom-BAH
cre----------a - tivity!
Koom-BAH, Koom-BAH
cre----------a - tivity!
Shape up!
Clean up!

Ee-MAH-nee   IMANI
---- All about faith
Ee-MAH-nee
---- All about faith
Ee-MAH-nee
---- All about faith
---- About faith

----Faith----
Believe it!

• In preparation for the remaining strategies, collect old magazines and the multiples of coupons they will need for the counting exercises. You will need about eight (nane) sheets of tag board for each student, approximately 8½" x 11" and a glue stick for each pair of students.

• Have each student find a picture of an object she or he likes. Students then paste that picture within an inch or two of the top of the tag board. At the top of the page students write "moja # one" (one apple, or whatever the item is). At the bottom, the student writes, "Umoja," day one of Kwanzaa.

```
┌─────────────────────────────────────┐
│                                      │
│       Moja # one; one apple          │
│                                      │
│                                      │
│                                      │
│                                      │
│     Umoja: day one of Kwanzaa        │
│                                      │
└─────────────────────────────────────┘
```

• Students then find two alike items that they value; paste them side by side in upper left quadrant of a new sheet of tag board. That sheet is labeled "mbili # two; two wheels", and "Kujichagulia, day two of Kwanzaa."

```
┌─────────────────────────────────────┐
│                                      │
│      mbili # two; two wheels         │
│                                      │
│                                      │
│                                      │
│                                      │
│    Kujichagulia, day two of Kwanzaa  │
│                                      │
└─────────────────────────────────────┘
```

• Following this pattern, each student works his/her way up to seven:

tanu # three	Ujima, day three
nne # four	Ujamaa, day four
tano # five	Nia, day five
sita # six	Kuumba, day six
saba # seven	Imani, day seven

or beyond:

nane # eight
tisa # nine
Kumi # ten

• Bind the eight sheets along one edge to make a booklet. Holes into which yarn is threaded will suffice. Or, in anticipation of adding other pages, they could be kept in folders. As students prepare to decorate the cover (eighth sheet), steer them toward textiles. Your library may have books that depict the effective way African cultures use fabrics for adornment and aesthetic appreciation.

STRATEGY:

What gives a thing its value? Explore the question through *The Black Snowman* by Phil Mendez; illustrated by Carol Byard.

Synopsis: The snowman they make is grimy, like that part of the city Jacob and Peewee live in. Jacob, older of two brothers, views the snowman as further proof that black is ugly. When a discarded remnant of kente cloth is draped around him, the black snowman comes to life — a reincarnation of the African griot. But Jacob is unbelieving, cynical, until the snowman marshalls the powers passed down the centuries from Africa to African America to help Jacob save his brother's life.

ACTIVITIES:

• Encourage the children to sing "Seven Principles", using the recording as background if necessary.

• Introduce students to new vocabulary; then invite discussion about the book title and cover illustration. (I mean, who ever heard of a *black* snowman! Really!)

• Read the story aloud. Alternatively, a parent or caring member of the community could be the reader. This would be an especially selected reader, one willing to become familiar with the story ahead of time. The story engages in a bit of fantasy. Why not imagine that you could get an African American fire fighter (male) to do the reading? What about a weaver? At the very minimum, your reader should wear a kente cloth strip.

• Encourage the children to speculate about the power remaining in the kente cloth: In what way might it affect the fire fighter's little girl? What will the doll look like? What will it do when clothed in the kente dress? Emphasize the value invested in the cloth. Questions about the origin of kente should encourage individual (or group) reading of *Huggy Bean and the Origin of the Magic Kente Cloth,* by Linda Cousins, and the first portrait in *Ashanti to Zulu* by Margaret Musgrove.

• Steer discussion back to how the fire fighter's daughter will get the kente piece: Imagine the fire fighter's daughter asking her grandmother (or the mother of her church) for help. What might the grandmother do with the pieces of cloth remaining after the doll's dress is finished?

• Work at getting children to understand that the cloth is invested with value because of who touches it and how they allow it to touch them. It would be appropriate here to have the students develop their own definitions of UJAMAA, such as that found in "How to Practice 'Nguzo Saba'" (see p. 15). Discuss with them, the Ashanti weavers' practice of naming kente cloth designs *(Ashanti to Zulu)*.

> UJAMAA (OO - JAH - MAH: COOPERATIVE ECONOMICS). One person alone may not have a lot; but when each person puts in her share of work, wealth, and will-power, everybody has more. (From "How to Practice Nguzo Saba")

STRATEGY:

Examine quilt making as a medium for development of stories, as in *"The Patchwork Quilt,"* by Valerie Flourney; illustrated by Jerry Pinkney.

Synopsis: Tanya's Grandma begins a quilt with scraps from clothing discarded by each member of the family. As family members are drawn into the project, Tanya comes to understand that *old* and *worn* can still be beautiful and valuable, because when united by loving hands, the quilt tells the story of her family.

ACTIVITIES:

• Persuade one or more parents, et al, to show your students quilts they have made or quilts that have passed through generations to them. They may wish to show off the never-used quilts locked in the bottom of trunks. Go with the flow, but make sure that well-used quilts get equal billing.
• Have the quilt custodians discuss what went into the making of each quilt. Perhaps articles of clothing (and the wearers of that clothing) can be identified. Call attention to shapes, fabrics, textures, colors, stitching — whatever might give viewers clues to the memories captured in the quilts.
• Introduce new vocabulary. Read the book to the students, or consider giving the pleasure to a parent capable of an intimate reading.
• Play the Bill Withers recording "Grandma's Hands." Encourage students to sing along.
• Encourage students to re-examine the quilts. Each student should select sections or pieces that interest her/him. The adults can help students speculate about the person who wore the garments or hung the drapes from which the quilt pieces came.
• Each student then constructs a profile of the garment-wearer. Students may choose to model their garment-wearer after characters in the books, or teachers, or family members. But they can go beyond that when compelled to deal with such lead questions as:
  1) When did the person live? In what year was she born?
  2) Was my school here at that time? Could he have / did he

21

attend this school?

3) When he was the same age as me, what did he most like to do?

4) What was the garment she wore before a piece of it became part of this quilt? How well did she take care of the garment?

5) What did other people say when they saw her wearing it?

6) In what way did her life begin to be different after she stopped wearing it?

7) Why did he stop wearing the garment? What did he do and where did he do it after he put the garment aside?

• Students write drafts of their profiles, embellishing them with drawings, bits of cloth, etc; then revise and finish the products.

• The finished products are gathered in with your help, students will see that they have created an extended family. They will have worked together in the spirit of Ujamaa. They will have given substance to the concept of multiculturalism.

• Give the family something to do, like coming together for a wedding, a christening of a newborn, paying tribute to an elder. Ultimately, engage your students in planning a reunion for this multicultural family. You could even call the reunion, "Karamu."

POSTSCRIPT:

Let the word "masterpiece" roll around among your students. Emphasize that creation of a masterpiece is more likely to result from preparation, cooperation, time on task, attitude, passion, all in balance:

> KUUMBA (koo-oom-bah) CREATIVITY. I create plans for a good home and a good school and a good community...I can create beautiful things, and I will, because inside I am a beautiful person. (From "How to Practice Nguzo Saba.")

STRATEGY:

Connect valuing, wisdom and self-determination through *The Hundred Penny Box* by Sharon Bell Mathis, illustrated by Leo and Diane Dillon.

> Synopsis: Eight year old Michael loves his 30 year old mother, Ruth. He loves his great-great aunt, Aunt Dew. But Aunt Dew's cracked-up, wacky-dacky box," holding only a sack of 100 pennies, is sort of in the way. Unlike Michael, Ruth has not heard the story behind each penny — one for each year of Aunt Dew's life. She wants to replace the big box with a shiny, neat one just big enough to hold the sack of pennies. Michael has a tough job trying to get his mother to understand how precious the hundred penny box is.

ACTIVITIES:

Parents read THE HUNDRED PENNY BOX and zero in on the intimate conversation between John Boy (Michael) and Aunt Dew: "He touched her arms: 'Are your arms a hundred years old?' he asked... 'Is your face and your eyes and fingers a hundred years old, too?' " *Discuss this with your child. Help the child consider that although Aunt Dew's 100 year old fingers no longer make quilts, she still creates story.*

• Before the lesson begins, ask parents (your colleagues, too) to help your students collect pennies. Each student needs the number of pennies equivalent to her/his age. Ideally, the dates stamped on the pennies would correspond to each year of the student's life: a child born in 1981 and now ten years old would have pennies for 1981, and each year thereafter up to 1991. Each child's collection can be stored in an envelope with his/her name on it.

• Also ask parents to try to reconstruct a chronology of major events in their children's lives. For example: 1981 christening; 1982 first tooth; first steps, 1984; first haircut, 1987; blew out candles on birthday cake, 1988. Ask parents to discuss the chronology with their children.

• Lastly, seek the cooperation of the person that cleans your classroom. You will be making a time line of pennies on the floor that should not be disturbed for a couple of days; thus the need for that person's cooperation. The custodian may need to know that, too, lest he or she reprimand the cleaning person.

• As the new words are introduced, make special efforts to link "penny" and "precious." It might help to demonstrate the buying power of a penny, or even 100 pennies.

• Discuss the potential value of 100 pennies. Compare a 1981 penny — perhaps the year most of your students were born — to the first square sewed into Tanya's quilt: isolated, neither has much value; united through an act of love the innocuous becomes precious.

• Play a recording of "Take My Hand, Precious Lord." Ask the students what kind of person might have composed it, and under what circumstances. Play the recording again, encouraging students to concentrate on how the composer felt.*

Help students evoke how they felt when they were lost and eager for someone to "take my hand." Discuss the lyric's, i.e., "I am weak. I am worn" (p. 14). Start the recording again, but lower the volume as you begin reading *The Hundred Penny Box.*

• Use a resource person for each subsequent reading. Be sure to have the new reader(s) recap what the previous reader covered. Pause before the second reading. Ask students to close their eyes and listen for raindrops beating against the window. After a moment have the reader begin.

---

* See the 1983 film, "Say Amen Somebody." Also available on video through Pacific Arts Video and Records.

ENRICHMENT:

Discussion should center on topics such as:

1) Why Ruth wants to get rid of "that big old ugly wooden box always under foot!" (p. 15)

2) What Ruth does not know about Aunt Dew's need to hold onto the box: "she will hold onto everything that is hers - just to hold on to them" (p. 36).

3) How Aunt Dew describes her need to hold on to the box: "I got to keep looking at my box and when I don't see my box, I won't see me neither" (p. 25, also see p. 37 for Michael's view).

4) The challenge Michael faces: "Michael was beginning to feel desperate. But he couldn't tell Aunt Dew what his mother said" (p. 25).

5) Have the students form a time line on the floor using the pennies that have been collected. The pennies should be touching each other, and taped to the floor. Let the time line remain for a couple of days, making it necessary for everyone to be careful, "lest it (the pennies) disappear."

6) Engage students in creating *Habari Gani* (What's the News) *Journal.* Each student would write a "news" story around one or more of the events the parents included in the chronology of their children's lives. This could be a cooperative learning project in which students share perspectives on the year and the significance of the event. Library research, especially review of encyclopedia yearbooks, would enable students to tie their selected events to world-shaping events. Again, selected resource persons may be willing to share rich anecdotes based on their experiences in the years selected by students. Each student's composition becomes an entry for the *Habari Gani Journal.* You could also encourage entries from parents and other resource persons. They could contribute one page summaries of their participation in the class-centered Kwanzaa activities.

7) Mapping Aunt Dew's character results in her being designated a self-determining person — one who exemplifies Kujichagulia.

> KUJICHAGULIA (koo-jee-chah-goo-LEE-ah) SELF-DETERMINATION. It seems hard to say, but I try and try to learn it; and I learn that it's about making up my mind to "keep on keeping on" in everything I do (from "How to Practice Nguzo Saba.").

TABONO
(Paddle)
Symbol of Strength, Confidence and Persistence.

Breaking Bread - Pen and ink. Ademola Olugebefola (Courtesy Grinnell Gallery) from Kwanzaa: Everything You Always Wanted To Know But Didn't Know Where To Ask by Cedric McClester, Gumbs & Thomas Publishers, New York.

CHAPTER **3**
(tanu)

The "Harvest" Concept in the Kwanzaa Holiday: A Theme Unit For Youths

DESCRIPTION:

This unit is designed to motivate students to apply the core ideas of Kwanzaa to the way they function in their own families, and to enhance their appreciation of the inter-relatedness of diverse groups. Students and their teachers will be able to plan and implement:

1) an in-school assembly to introduce other students to Kwanzaa.
2) a Karamu, i.e., evening of celebration to which family and community members are invited.

Though a single teacher can implement this unit, it is desirable and logical that a cluster of teachers practice Ujima — collective work and responsibility; and Ujamaa — cooperative economics.

Stories are drawn from three trade books: *Have a Happy . . .* , a novel; *Ashanti to Zulu,* a picture book with brief descriptions of 26 African cultures; and "Graduation," Chapter 23 of *I Know Why the Caged Bird Sings.* * The novel and picture books are read orally in class, over a number of sessions. You may choose to have "Graduation" read privately by each student. Ideally, students would read the selection in conjunction with their families. Again, a sensitive storyteller, steeped in African American traditions, can greatly enrich the unit.

---

* The entire book is valuable. Continue reading - cover to cover - into the new year. Alternatively, begin Chapter 1 early in the semester.

While not the subjects of this unit, tradebooks used in Chapter 2 can enrich your work with youths. Recommended are: *The Patchwork Quilt; The Black Snowman; The Hundred Penny Box; Moja Means One; Jambo Means Hello*. Also, *Listen for the Fig Tree*, by Sharon Bell Mathis, is an excellent novel (reading/interest level, grade 7 and above) that employs the Kwanzaa theme.

OBJECTIVES:

1) After listening to, reading and discussing three books, and, given participation in a workshop, the student will:
- decode new words
- identify, through mapping, the character traits of principal figures in two of the books
- assign to the novel and to "Graduation," Kwanzaa principles evident in these selections, and provide support for the choices

2) Given lessons on planning and decision making, the class will plan and implement a Karamu as a culminating activity.

3) Given instruction on appropriate forms and conventions in letter writing, the student will write and send a letter of invitation to at least one family member or surrogate.

4) Given participation in the Karamu, the student will write personal reactions and feelings regarding Kwanzaa into a report-letter to a relative for friend living outside the student's community.

STRATEGY:

Introduce the concept of "holiday" as *one or more days set aside by custom, whereby regular business is suspended in order to commemorate a special event, development or history*.

ACTIVITIES:

• Play the recording, "Seven Principles," by Sweet Honey in the Rock.

• Follow up with a definition of "commemorate"; emphasize the idea of honoring, as opposed to merely taking a day off to go shopping. Elicit examples of holidays in which the students and their families have actually commemorated a special event, development or history.

• Using "A Calendar of Religious Holidays and Ethnic Festivals" (National Council of Christians and Jews), United Nations Children's Fund Calendars or similar resources, discuss ethnic and religious holidays. Distinguish between commercial trappings and symbols grounded in core traditions.

• Conclude this introduction by announcing that *for the next several (number of days/weeks) we will set aside a portion of each (day/period) to study a seven day holiday. It is a holiday, born in this century, yet based on centuries' old traditions, rooted in harvest festivals.*

• Your version of the foregoing statement would be incorporated into your letter to parents, consistent with the recommendations cited in Chapter 2 under "Preparation" (p. 12). Have students deliver the letters as they follow through on engaging their family members, et al., in discussion of "holiday," and "gathering-in." (Build in a feedback element. Threaten to sneak a virus into their television sets so they can't be turned off, but run continuously, that same commercial about "deep discount" carpeting.) Point out that you are already in contact with resource persons who will enhance the in-school experience. Urge students to engage their parents, or other family and community members, in discussion of *holiday, harvest* and *commemoration.*

STRATEGY:

Search for the concept of *harvest* through *Have a Happy . . .* by Mildred Pitts Walter; illustrated by Carol Byard.

> Synopsis: Chris wonders "Why can't people just say 'have a happy?'". Then I could add anything I want: happy birthday, happy Christmas, happy Kwanzaa, or Happy New Year." Chris's December 25 birthday is always overshadowed by Christmas, but this year, even that may be spoiled, because Chris's father hasn't found a job. But Uncle Ronald and Grandma Ida hold the family together for the Kwanzaa celebration. As they concentrate on the principles, the family's fortunes begin to change.

ACTIVITIES:

• Play the recording, "Seven Principles," encouraging the students to sing along.
• Distribute copies of *Have a Happy . . .* Describe it as a novel about Kwanzaa — a seven day celebration of the gathering-in of people.
• Present vocabulary, emphasizing the italicized words in the text. Have students practice vowel sounds as explained in the glossary. Explain that the Kwanzaa words are drawn from Kiswahili, an East African language. Reinforce through use of *Mojo Means One* and *Jambo Means Hello* (see Chapter 2, "Kiswahili: Introducing the language through picture books...").
• Read the first chapter to the students. Invite discussion: call attention to the out-of-work father, but help students see that subject as common to many real-life families. Emphasize Daddy's pride and the extraordinary lengths to which he goes in search of employment. Point out that Chris, like Daddy, makes efforts to keep the relationship positive.
[• As an outside class assignment you will have each student develop a list of members of his/her own nuclear family, including members living in different households, away at college, etc.
After students read Chapter 2, ask them about Uncle Ronald's experience 29

in Ghana: Where is Ghana? What would people there likely harvest as "first fruits?"* Later, require that students expand their lists of family members to include aunts, uncles and their offspring, and grandparents, especially if they reside in homes separate from that of the students. Include city and state for each relative.]

• Close the session with students' oral reading of Chapter 2 (mbili) of *Have a Happy . . .* (In anticipation of subsequent strategies secure a number of road maps of the major regions of this country. Friends with membership in automobile travel clubs should be solicited. Plan to divide the class into cooperative learning groups based on the regions one or more of their extended family members lives in. Examples: Northeast, Mid-Atlantic).

STRATEGY: Display the Kwanzaa ritual symbols:

bendera (ben-deh-dah): flag
kikombe (kee-koám-bay): cup
kikombe cha umoja (kee-koám-bay chah oo-moe-jah: unity cup
kinara (kee-nah-rah): candle holder
mazao (mah-zah-oh): crops
mkeka (m-kay-cah): straw mat
mishumaa (mee-shoo-maah): candles
mishumaa saba (mee-shoo-maah sah-bah): seven candles
muhindi (moo-heen-dee): ears of corn
zawadi (zah-wah-dee): gift of gifts

ACTIVITIES:

• Have three students read aloud, Chapters 2, 3 and 4 of *Have a Happy...*
• Initiate discussion, encouraging students to compare Chris's family to their own. Focus on Uncle Ronald, "already thirty" (p. 12), yet the youngest of four: two sisters and two brothers."
• Discuss why Uncle Ronald and Grandma Ida live in different households.
• Call attention to Grandma coming over to fix breakfast, and taking Beth with her so that Mama and Chris are free to concentrate on their work. Indicate that this is an act of Ujima — collective work and responsibility — the third of seven principles that comprise Nguzo (n-goo-zoe) Saba (sah-bah).
• Print the third principle — Ujima — and its English equivalent in large letters on a card (about 3" x 15"), and tape it to a conspicuous place. Do this for principles 2 and 3, and for the other principles as the discussion focuses on them.
• Encourage students to learn the song, "Seven Principles." It's a foregone conclusion that a core group, if not the entire class will want to perform the song at Karamu.

* Reference to a "celebration called kwanza" (lower case 'k', word ending with a single 'a'), may be the author's invention. In the Kiswahili language, "kwanza" means "first". Ghana is in West Africa and the people are likely to refer to their harvest festival fruits in a language common to them.

STRATEGY:

Diversity among the peoples of Africa, as depicted in *Ashanti to Zulu* by Margaret Musgrove; illustrated by Leo and Diane Dillon.

> Synopsis: The writer and two illustrators combine their talents to produce picture and word portraits of 26 cultural groups dispersed across Africa. The text of the one page devoted to Ashanti is exclusively about the weavers of kente.

ACTIVITIES:

- Use this opportunity to bring in resource people:
  - African living, working, attending college among Americans.
  - A former Peace Corps volunteer sharing what he learned about the people in whose country he served.
  - A museum educator bringing artifacts to the school.
  - A field trip to the museum.
  - Kente cloth — that marvelous, steeped in tradition fabric woven by Ashanti men. (Strips of it are regularly imported and sold in some retail outlets).
- Have a parent do an oral reading to the class of *The Black Snowman* (see Synopsis of p. 20 of this book).
- Walk students through *Ashanti to Zulu*. The people depicted in this book could be referred to as "black," yet each has a name and a style of living that is unique to each group. By naming themselves and practicing their cultures, each group is expressing Kujichagulia — self determination. Encourage students to ponder specific practices: Why in Ga tradition is the right hand designated as the one to touch food?
- Refer to the map on the last page of *Ashanti to Zulu*. Have each student print on a political map the name of each of the groups cited in the book. Have the students do library research to help them identify some of the political, historical and economic (trade and commerce) factors the group have to contend with.

STRATEGY:

Greet students with "Habari Gani?" (hah-bah-dee gah-nee), i.e., "What's the news?"

ACTIVITIES:

- Have students turn to the Swahili Glossary (p. 85) in *Have a Happy* . . Repeat the greeting, "Habari Gani," and have them read the response "Kwanzaa yenu iwe na heri" (Kwanzaa - yay-noo eeway nah heh-dee) — "Happy Kwanzaa." Repeat the sequence several times.
- Show the filmstrip "Kwanzaa: An Afro-American Holiday."
- Have a student read Chapter 6 of *Have a Happy* . . . to the class. Place

the discussion in the context of the student's efforts to create their lists of kin, and the reasons relatives live in different locations.

STRATEGY:

Have a student read Chapter 7 (saba) and another student read Chapter 8 (nane) of *Have a Happy . . .*

ACTIVITIES:

• Discuss both chapters, concentrating on Chris's feelings: "Unable to stand the sad, worried look on his father's face, Chris turned away..." (p. 44). "Chris went home feeling more worried and afraid than ever." (p. 55)
Contrast these feelings with the dialogue between Chris, Miles and Jamal on page 46:

"My whole family goes," Miles said.

"My family's just me and my mama," Jamal said softly.

"Not at Kwanzaa," Chris said. "Everybody is your family at Kwanzaa, right Miles?"

"But you have to go to know. We're going tonight," Miles said.

• Discuss separation from family and home in an historical context. Speculate as to how many of the *Ashanti to Zulu* groups may have lost people to the Atlantic slave trade:

"It's likely that all the groups were affected, but the heaviest toll would fall on the West African groups: Dogon, Vai, Ashanti, Baule, Ga, Fanti, Ewe, Yoruba, Uge, Hausa, Ndaka, Wagenia, Quimbande, and Kung. Yet these represented only a fraction of the groups that lost their brightest and strongest people to the African slave trade."

• Make the point that the difficulty in getting accurate information on our extended family members living in other states is minuscule compared to that African Americans face in trying to trace their ancestry to one of the *Ashanti to Zulu* groups.

"Descendants of Africans in America — African Americans — are dispersed. Yet those descendants have a marvelous history to celebrate; a history that gives texture and color to the history of the Americas, even as its roots are in Africa. Kwanzaa calls on dispersed people to gather-in."

Parents and children engage in developing lists of relatives. Discuss the kinship lines in order to identify the earliest known relative (forebear).
(For sessions 7 and 8, you will need a large outline map of North and South America, Europe, Africa, and the western extremities of Asia — the areas with deepest involvement in the Atlantic slave trade. Make a transparency of the map printed at the end of this session. Use an overhead projector to project the image onto a large expanse (perhaps 50" x 100") of paper taped to the walls in the corridors. Trace the image in pencil; then retrace the pencil lines with a broad tip, dark-colored marker.

STRATEGY:

Greet students with "Habari Gani?" to elicit the response "Kwanzaa yenu iwe na heri."

ACTIVITIES:

• Have the students report on the making of the lists of their relatives. Progress will be mixed. Talk about the challenge as an effort to gather-in, i.e., to harvest — an exercise in cooperative economics (Ujamaa):

> To make use of, to profit from the gathering of names, addresses, relationships, calls for cooperation within one's family members. It is, in a word, *harambee* (hah-rahm-bay) — "Let's all pull together."

• Lead students in expressing harambee as a call for pulling together: Raise one open hand a few inches above your head as if about to grasp the support rail (or loop) provided for standing bus passengers. Pull down sharply as you close your hand into a fist, while articulating (roll those "r's"), "Harambee." Raise the open hand again and repeat the gesture. Do this five more times. For the seventh harambee, hold the first two syllables about ten seconds: "Ha-ram-m-m-m..." before pulling the fist down sharply on "...bee!".

• Three students, in rotation, conclude reading of *Have a Happy...* Chapters 9 (tisa), 10 (kumi) and 11 (kumi na moja).

• As suggested earlier, students should be organized into cooperative learning groups, more or less according to the region in which selected relatives reside. Using rulers, pencil, paper, and the road maps (all drawn to the same scale), students can estimate mileage from their home to each relative's location. Key cities can be printed on your map and lines of yarn connecting your school and the city nearest each relative.

Parents, having read the selections, and engaged your students in discussion of "commemoration," you are well prepared to appraise Maya Angelou's achievements. You can help your students appreciate their opportunities to achieve.

ENRICHMENT:

This activity can be extended using a different color of yarn to connect your locale to those areas labeled on the *Ashanti to Zulu* map.

• Challenge students to estimate cost, time, transportation, room and board, and other factors that would go into visiting one of the remote sites, or having the relative visit your school.

STRATEGY: Develop A Process For "gathering-in", i.e. a Karamu

ACTIVITIES:

• Have students, in teams, role play Chapter 8 of *Have a Happy...*, the celebration at Uncle Ronald's house. You may wish to simplify the task by omitting (or making a substitution) Chris's uneasiness: "...feeling more worried and afraid than ever" (p. 55).

• Each role play should be critiqued, keeping the focus on how the entire class can make the scene clear and alive to an audience that has not had your students' experiences. You may wish to use a "cued and free retelling" technique to help the groups rehearse the scene. In this technique, students work in pairs. One is given one or more "Free and Cued Retelling" (p. 53) sheets. Under "Story Cues," I print bits of action from the story. One student is asked to tell as much of the story as she/he can, in her/his own words. When the teller gets stuck, the listener offers a cue and puts a check in the the right-hand column. After one or two tellings, they switch roles.

• After each team has experienced one role play and critique, do a general critique allowing individuals to demonstrate how particular roles can be portrayed. Variations are acceptable. After general consensus, shift to the actual planning of the Karamu.

• Distribute copies of "Karamu Planning Outline" (p. 54). Allow intergroup discussion of the description of karamu,, writing conclusions on large sheets of paper. Consensus should come at some point, and that single description taped to the wall. For items 2, 3, 4 and 5, a wider range of recommendations will likely be produced. If you also require a rationale for each recommendation, students will be compelled to be more thoughtful; thus, a modest number of "best" ideas will go on the sheets of paper. When all recommendations are taped to the wall, discuss need, feasibility and appropriateness, in order to arrive at a preliminary plan, i.e., things needed; steps to be carried out; other things to be considered; and program needs.

STRATEGY: Fine tune and rehearse the Karamu plan.

On page 41 is an outline of a six component "Karamu Program Format." McClester's *Kwanzaa: Everything You Always Wanted to Know But Didn't Know Where to Ask* has another version. Karenga provides a detailed comprehensive description in the *African American Holiday of Kwanzaa*. Whatever components your students select for their Karamu should be pursued with care and taste.

ACTIVITIES:

• Using the "Student-Led Assembly" (p. 35) as a guide, tailor a script to your student's abilities and to the circumstances that prevail in your school.

• Assign parts and rehearse: making adjustments, switching roles if necessary. Make rehearsals part of each session.

• Present each student with a copy of the plan, including individual assignments and due dates. Insist on progress reports.

• Have students generate criteria for who is to be invited to the Karamu. If you have kept parents informed, more of them will be in a position to make contributions. Ask that each bring a dish of food to pass. Perhaps some can be persuaded to demonstrate a traditional dance; put up decorations; transport elders, etc.

- Present the format for the letter, but encourage personalization.
- Have students write letters; after each is properly addressed and mailed, make one or two students responsible for monitoring and tabulating responses.

STRATEGY: Plan for "A Student-Led Assembly" as a tune-up for Karamu.

ACTIVITIES:

[Off Stage: Fourteen students assemble in two equal groups at rear of auditorium. Others stand at attention on stage.]

[On Stage: A low (kindergarten?) table is set with the Kwanzaa implements: mkeka (straw mat), kinara and mishumaa (candle holder with three red, three green and one black candle); mazao (fruit and nuts); muhindi (ears of corn, possibly one for each member of the class); zawadi (gifts, e.g., one or more attractive books); kikombe cha umoja (the unity cup).]

FIRST NARRATOR: Kwanzaa is a seven day holiday, celebrating African American culture. On December 26 through January 1, African Americans who celebrate Kwanzaa call special attention to what they have done and what they will do, to make their community, schools, and country better. Kwanzaa is based on seven principles or main ideas.

[From the rear and on opposite sides of the auditorium, two groups of students chant a rap cadence while marching in lock step to the stage. The group of seven on the left call out the rap; the group of seven on the right respond, chanting exactly what they hear. They alternate; this time the group on the right is the caller; the left group is the responder. For example:

LEFT: Umoja! Umoja! Umoja! Umoja!
RIGHT: Umoja! Umoja! Umoja! Umoja!
LEFT: Ce-lebrate Umo-ja!
RIGHT: Ce-lebrate Umo-ja!

RIGHT: Ku-jichagu-lii-a!
LEFT: Ku-jichagu-lii-a!
RIGHT: Ku-jichagu-lii-a!
LEFT: Ku-jichagu-lii-a!

This continues until both groups are on stage. After going through the seven principles, they repeat "Imani" until everyone is in a single straight line.

[Different student steps forward exhorting audience to "pump it up!" (or some such command.) Entire class now becomes callers of the rap (above) and audience members the responders.]

35

CALL: U-mo-ja! U-mo-ja! U-mo-ja! U-mo-ja!
RESPONSE: U-mo-ja! U-mo-ja! U-mo-ja U-mo-ja!
CALL: Ce-le-brate Umoja!
RESPONSE: Ce-le-brate Umoja!
[Students part, stand to either side of table.]

SECOND NARRATOR: On December 26, the black candle is lighted.
It is black because it represents the people.
It also stands for the first principle, Umoja.

UMOJA STUDENT: Umoja means unity . . .
(Student completes statement with an appropriate interpretation.)

[Light black candle]

Umoja. *Unity.*

KUJICHAGULIA STUDENT: Kujichagulia. Self determination . . .
(Student completes statement with an appropriate interpretation.)

[Light one red candle.]

Kujichagulia. *Self-determination.*

UJIMA STUDENT: Ujima. *Collective work and responsibility* . . .
(Student completes statement with an appropriate interpretation.)

[Light one green candle.]

Ujima. *Collective Economics.*

UJAMAA STUDENT: Ujamaa. *Cooperative Economics...*
(Student completes statement with an appropriate interpretation.)

[Light one red candle.]

Ujamaa. *Collective Economics.*

NIA STUDENT: Nia. *Purpose* . . .
(Student completes statement with an appropriate interpretation.)

[Light one green candle.]

Nia. *Purpose.*

KUUMBA STUDENT: Kuumba. *Creativity* . . .
(Student completes statement with an appropriate interpretation.)

[Light one red candle.]

Kuumba. *Creativity.*

IMANI STUDENT: Imani. *Faith.* . .
(Student completes statement with an appropriate interpretation.)

[Light one green candle.]

Imani. *Faith.*

THIRD NARRATOR: The Kwanzaa holiday is celebrated December 26 through January 1, but we can live the seven principles every day of the year.

FOURTH NARRATOR: Now we present a scene showing how one family celebrated Umoja, the first night of Kwanzaa. The players are: Chris, a boy eleven years old, who . . .
[Chris steps forward to describe his character.]

FOURTH NARRATOR: Beth is Chris's younger sister.
[Beth steps forward to describe her character.]

FOURTH NARRATOR: Uncle Ronald . . .
                Mama . . .
                Miles . . .
                Jamal . . .
                Daddy . . .
                Grandma Ida . . .

(Each character, in turn, describes himself/herself to the audience. Use as many or as few characters as desired.)

[As characters arrange themselves and the few props, the narrator sets the scene. Props would include the table with its Kwanzaa implements, decorations or illustrations students have created. For example, early involvement of your art teacher could enable students to produce large portraits of the heroic figures named in the *tamshi la tambiko* (p. 53 of *Have a Happy...*): Malcolm X, Martin Luther King, Jr., Medgar Evers, Mary Church Terrel, Fannie Lou Hamer, and Ida B. Wells.]

NARRATOR: It gets next to Chris to hear all his friends bragging about the Christmas presents they expect to get. Chris was born on Christmas Day and has no hope of having a birthday properly celebrated. I mean, how can an eleven-year old boy compete with the son of God? Besides, Chris's father is out of work. But Uncle Ronald gathers the whole family — aunts, uncles, cousins, Grandma Ida, and a bunch of friends — for celebration of Kwanzaa. Everybody has a role and a responsibility, so Chris has less time to feel sorry for himself. In this scene, we find everybody gathered at Uncle Ronald's house for the first night of Kwanzaa, called Umoja.

[Thereafter, the students re-enact their version of Chapter 8 of *Have a Happy*] Conclude the assembly with a spirited singing of "Lift Every Voice and Sing."

STRATEGY: Autobiography as illustration of values inherent in Kwanzaa.

Preparation: Maya Angelou's autobiography exhibits candor, strength, wit, optimism and verve. These qualities are consistent with Nguzo Saba. On the next page is a short essay on Chapter 23 of Angelou's *I Know Why the Caged Bird Sings*. Read it with the students, as background for Angelou's piece. In addition to student copies of Chapter 23, students should have access to the following:

MAYA ANGELOU: *Poems*, a Bantam Books publication, 1986.

"O BLACK AND UNKNOWN BARDS": Poem by James Weldon Johnson, in various anthologies.

"LIFT EVERY VOICE AND SING": Poem by James Weldon Johnson and set to music by J. Rosamond Johnson. A good background on the creation of "Lift Every Voice and Sing," is in Jane Tolbert-Rouchaleau's *James Weldon Johnson*, published by Chelsea House, 1988.

MAYA ANGELOU'S SCHOOL EXPERIENCE AS
REFERENCE POINT FOR KWANZAA:
(An Essay on "Graduation" from Angelou's Autobiography,
I Know Why the Caged Bird Sings)

Graduation, even from eighth grade, calls for celebration. But young Maya has larger reasons than has Chris, to be worried and anxious about the future. She attended a school that had few of the things we take for granted. The school system that ran the school was bossed by white men who saw it as their duty to withold support for the all-Black school Maya attended. These were the days of racial segregation.

It was as if African American children had been assigned a permanent condition of inferiority: something like AIDS, except this disease attacked the mind and spirit. Should an African American adult openly demonstrate that she or he was a citizen, therefore, entitled to a citizen's rights, that adult could lose his job, even his life. The law did not protect him or her.

The laws of several states were designed to deny African American children opportunity for quality schooling. In spite of such handicaps, Maya and her schoolmates worked hard. They respected each other. They respected their teachers, and their teachers respected them and taught them well. The children's parents wanted them to learn, and they supported the teachers' efforts to teach their children. Students, teachers, and families worked at unity of purpose.

Chapter 23 of Maya Angelou's autobiography, *I Know Why the Caged Bird Sings*, begins on a happy note. But, evil, in the guise of an official of the uncaring school system, casts an ugly shadow across the sunshine of Maya's graduation celebration. Unity begins to slip away from the African American parents, teachers, and students. Their noble purpose is about to crumble. The values planted in Maya and the other children by their parents and teachers are pressed into the lowest recesses of their being. Yet, having reached bottom, they begin to reach out for each other, and as Angelou expressed in a recent poem, "Up from the past that's rooted in pain, I rise."*

ACTIVITIES:

Parents read the essay about Maya Angelou's autobiography (above), Read Chapter 23 of I KNOW WHY THE CAGED BIRD SINGS (Maya Angelou). Also consult LIFT EVERY VOICE AND SING (Mozell Thompson), and JAMES WELDON JOHNSON (Janet Tolbert-Rochaleau). These biographical materials portray two individuals who set aside regular business in order to commemorate a special event, development or history.

• Introduce new vocabulary.
• Set the scene. Tell students that this is Angelou's account of a very challenging part of her childhood in Stamps, Arkansas, around 1940. Help students locate Stamps on a map. (It's about 150 miles southwest of Little Rock, and 30 miles east of Texarkana, a small city on the Texas-Arkansas border.)
• Tell students that in 1940 the laws of some states allowed local school districts to segregate students by race; that even though the United States Constitution "guaranteed" African Americans equal protection, the federal government allowed the states to discriminate.
• Have students read "Graduation" silently (or possibly to someone at home). In discussion, identify theme, mood, plot, conflict. Point out Maya's attention to the details of everyone getting ready to celebrate; how she felt she was the center of everyone's attention; her sense of receiving special, holy blessings:

"I . . . thanked God that no matter what evil I had done in my life, He had allowed me to live to see this day. Somewhere in my fatalism I had expected to die, accidentally, and never have the chance to . . . gracefully receive my hard-earned diploma. Out of God's merciful bosom I had won reprieve" (p. 170).

• Walk your students through that moment of apprehension:

"Something unrehearsed, unplanned was going to happen, and we were going to be made to look bad" (p. 172).

---

*The poem, "And Still I Rise" deserves a full reading. Students would greatly benefit from a performance reading by one of Angelou's many admirers. See *Maya Angelou: Poems,* Bantam Books, New York, 1986.

• Bring them to the fulfillment of Donleavy's put-down (pp. 174, 175) and Maya's near capitulation to the urge to embrace bitterness and contempt for herself and her race:

"...As a species we were an abomination. All of us" (p. 176).

• Finally, try to get the students to put themselves in that school on that day. Let them see the Nguzo Saba resurrected as Henry Reed

". . . turn(ed) his back to the audience and turn(ed) to us . . . and sing, nearly speaking, "Lift ev'ry voice and sing, Till earth and heaven ring, Ring with the harmonies of Liberty..." (p. 178).

• Present a list of Angelou's credentials. Point out that despite having her schooling interrupted several times, she is today a distinguished professor of humanities at a prestigious university. Emphasize that none of her great accomplishments would have occured had she not been open to discovering life every day.

ENRICHMENT:

In December 1990, two teachers of Douglass Middle School (Rochester, New York) students involved 18 students in a unit on Kwanzaa. Nancy Sundberg and Ruth Anderson challenged their students to describe Nguzo Saba in their words. Below is a sampling of their interpretations. Have your students critique the work of the Frederick Douglass students. Have them write their own interpretations. After compiling and editing the results, transform them into posters (as suggested in Chapter 2, p. 10), or place mats. Also have each student print interpretations on 3" x 5" cards. You should mail these to parents, requesting that they post them in conspicuous places in the home.

Parents use magnets to attach these cards to the refrigerator.

UMOJA (oo-MOE-jah) UNITY
"You see Umoja when people are cooperating, working together, or learning together. When we work together, our Reading Workshop is a beautiful example of Umoja." (Demar Jackson, Fontaine Brooks, Ian Cortex, Del Johnson, Howard Robinson, Laquinda Dorsey)

KUJICHAGULIA (koo-jee-CHA-goo-lee-ah) SELF DETERMINATION
"When people are confident and determined to do something and they're not going to give up, no matter what, you see Kujichagulia. When I make myself a resolution or a goal and I carry out that goal, no matter how many times I have to try...it's showing Kujichagulia." (Nathaniel Heywood)

"Kujichagulia is like when Mr. Acongio said I had a 'meteoric rise' since I came to Douglass," (middle school) "and I know I'm in charge of my life." (Andre Cotto)

"When I make decisions for myself and don't follow the crowd, I'm showing Kujichagulia." (Sarah Tyler)

NIA (nee-AH) PURPOSE
"When people set a goal and work towards it, they are showing Nia. In my own life I show Nia when I maintain my goal to finish school so I can be somebody." (Christine Jamieson)

"When people know why they are living and they work to make a better world by and by...When I go to school, I go with the plan to graduate...That is Nia." (Dan Reid)

STRATEGY: Implementing Karamu

Parents gather photographs, letters and other items identified with relatives living in distant places. Arrange the items in one or more places where they can be seen. Write a sentence or a paragraph about each person on a card. Attach a colorful ribbon to each card. Hang the cards around, or near the items. Use these to start family members discussion of reasons that relatives live apart from each other.

Rehearsals continue; invitees respond; building permit came through approved. Everything unfolds exactly on schedule, right? Well, at least portions of your plan are hurtling down on you. You are not alone. I, too, am sweating out one.

KARAMU PROGRAM FORMAT

The essential components of a Kwanzaa celebration include 1) ritual; 2) information; 3) food; 4) decorative motif; 5) celebration of achievement designed to illustrate the principle of the day; 6) farewell statement.

Ritual
a. tribute to the forerunners (Tamshi la Tambiko)
b. pouring of libation (Tambiko), followed by seven harambees
c. lighting of mishumma (candles)
d. commemoration of notable event or life of person(s) that exemplified the principle of the day

Information
a. explanation of the meaning of each implement or symbol
b. announcements regarding other Kwanzaa events scheduled in community

Food
Each family is asked to bring a dish to pass (get commitments for specific items). **41**

a. pot luck is preferred, e.g., hoppin' john, Daufuskie stew.
    alternative: desserts, such as sweet potato pie, bean pie, deep dish pie, or other traditional foods
    alternative: hot buttermilk cornbread
    alternative: fruits, nuts

Decorative Motif
a. colors: red, green and black
b. corn, gourds, traditional harvest symbols

Celebration of Achievement
a. solos, dance, drama, poetry or other forms of inner-attainment
b. crafts and games
c. group singing (call and response)
d. testimonials

Farewell Statement (Tamshi La Tutaonana)
a. seven harambees

Adjust the format to suit your needs. The activities presented in the student-led assembly should be easy enough and fit under "Celebration of Achievement" and "Information." For the "Ritual" and "Farewell Statement", you should rely on a respected Kwanzaa devotee - a mature, secure African American adult. To the degree that he or she is say, under 50 years of age, it would be appropriate to call on an esteemed elder to assist in performing the ritual.

EVALUATION PROJECT

Objective:
    "...given participation in the culminating activity (Karamu), the student will record personal reactions or feelings regarding Kwanzaa into a report-letter to a friend or relative in another community."

Elements:
    The letter should follow the friendly letter form - return address, date, salutation, and inquiry into the health and well-being of the addressee. The body (see sample) of the letter should contain at least twelve paragraphs and a photograph:
    1) three or four sentences summarizing how the writer's Kwanzaa experience began, and led to the Karamu.
    2) description of Kwanzaa.
    3 - 9) one paragraph defines each of the principles (Kiswahili and English).
    10) which member(s) of student's family attended Karamu; how they participated, plus data on the photograph.
    11) summary of personal reflections.
    12) closing - whatever student wishes for the letter recipient in the way of Kwanzaa experiences or benefits.

SAMPLE CONTENT AND FORMAT FOR REPORT-LETTER

1) Last November M _____ introduced my class to Kwanzaa, the
   (teacher's name)

African American holiday. We read _____
                                        (book titles)

_____

and we _____ . On the

night before Christmas recess we had Karamu, which is _____ .

_____

2) Kwanzaa is...

   (Complete the sentence, then include more information such as dates, how
   Kwanzaa is celebrated, its principles, and symbols, etc.)

3) The first principle of Kwanzaa is _____ ,

   which means _____ .

4) The second principle of Kwanzaa is...

5) The third principle of Kwanzaa is...

6) The fourth principle of Kwanzaa is...

7) The fifth principle of Kwanzaa is...

8) The sixth principle of Kwanzaa is...

9) The seventh principle of Kwanzaa is...

   (Continue as in paragraph 2 above. Follow the same procedure for describ-
   ing each principle - a separate paragraph for each principle.)

10) My _____ and _____ came to the karamu. So did the _____

of the other students. We...

   (Tell some of what was done and by whom: food, ceremony, presentations,
   stories, mood of the group, etc.)

11) During our Kwanzaa project I have learned _____

_____ .

I enjoyed _____ .

   I would like to _____ .

If every student and teacher in our school, and all our families learned and prac-

ticed the principle, I think _____ .

   To me, Kwanzaa _____ .

12) Well, I hope _____ .

Please let me know _____ .

Yours truly, **43**

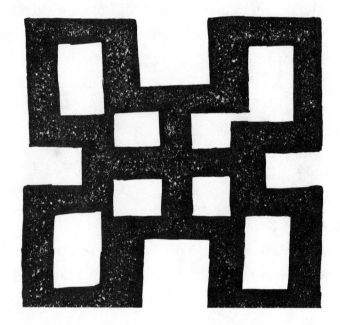

NSAA
Symbol of Excellence, Genuineness
and Authenticity.

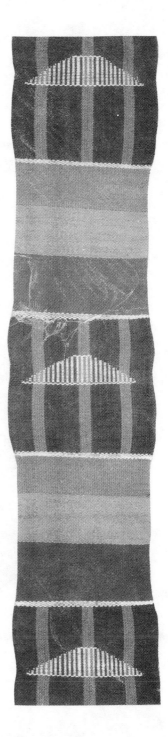

Afterword

OSRAM NE NSOROMMA
(Moon and Star)
Symbol of Faithfulness, Love, Harmony, fondness
Benevolence and Femininity.

More Words

Several places in this book refer to SANKOFA, a term I have attached to my surname. SANKOFA signifies the Akan proverb — go back and fetch what was left behind. The proverb guides me in my role as a traditional storyteller.

The African American lacks knowledge of specific African cultures, and is also woefully limited in knowledge of the African experience in America. But like Aunt Dew's penny box, and the snowman's scrap of kente, knowledge of beginnings is something precious, waiting for pilgrims to go back and fetch it.

In reaching back I have discovered that:
   Before there was Earth, there was Sky and far, far, far below Sky, water — only water. Sky was populated with would-be deities — would-be since there were no humans to deify them. One among them was of the essences, Curiosity and Creativity. It was that would-be deity who created Earth and its first inhabitants.

The foregoing summarizes a creation myth that I retell and will soon have in print. The substance of the story is based in an African culture. With such little knowledge of my African beginnings, I necessarily treat ancestral memories with respect. Yes, Kwanzaa too, celebrates beginnings, trials and potentials. So let us treat it with respect.

Kwanzaa: An Everyday Resource and Instructional Guide stops here. But like the story, we are at the beginning. Teachers in schools, homes and elsewhere who invite their students to learn and practice Nguzo Saba, are writing the next chapters.

KWANZAA yenu iwe na heri.

David A. Anderson/SANKOFA

NKYINKYMIIE
Symbol of Toughness, Adaptability,
Devotion to Service and Ability to
Withstand Hardships.

Appendix

Materials Used or Consulted

Primary Source Books for Chapter Two

Kwanzaa by Deborah M. Newton, Children's Press, Chicago, 1990.

* *The Patchwork Quilt* by Valerie Flourney, Dial Books for Young Readers, New York, 1985.

* *The Black Snowman* by Phil Mendez, Scholastic, New York, 1989.

* *The Hundred Penny box* by Sharon Bell Mathis, Puffin Books, New York, 1975.

Ashanti to Zulu by Margaret Musgrove, Dial Press, New York, 1976.

Moja Means One by Muriel Feelings, Dial Books for Young Readers, New York, 1971.

Jambo Means Hello by Muriel Feelings, Dial Books for Young Readers, New York, 1974.

Let's Celebrate Kwanzaa by Helen Davis Thompson, Gumbs & Thomas Publishers, New York, 1990.

Huggy Bean and the Origin of the Magic Kente Cloth by Linda Cousins, Gumbs & Thomas Publishers, New York, 1991.

Primary Source Books for Chapter Three (Youths)

* *Have a Happy...* by Mildred Pitts Walter, Avon Books, New York, 1989.

Ashanti to Zulu by Margaret Musgrove, Dial Press, New York, 1976.

* *I Know Why the Caged Bird Sings* by Maya Angelou, Random House, New York, 1969.

Secondary Source Books (Children and Youths)

Getting Ready for Kwanzaa by Margaret Bland, Jomar Enterprises, Seattle Washington, 1985.

* *Listen for the Fig Tree* by Sharon Bell Mathis, Puffin Books, New York, 1974.

Shake It To the One that You Love the Best by Cheryl Warren Mattox, Warren-Mattox Productions, 1989.

Ethnic Pride by Greta Lipson and Jane Romatowski, Good Apple, Inc., Carthage, Illinois, 1983.

African Textiles by John Picton and John Mack, Harper and Row, New York, 1989.

Faces: The Magazine About People, January, 1985, Cobblestone Publishing Co., Peterborough, New Hamphire.

United Nations Children's Fund Calendar, UNICEF, Chattanooga, Tennessee.

Calendar of Religious Holidays and Ethnic Festivals, National Council of Christians and Jews.

The African American Holiday of Kwanzaa by Maulana Karenga, University of Sankore Press, Los Angeles, California, 1988.

Kwanzaa: Everything You Wanted to Know But Didn't Know Where to Ask by Cedric McClester, Gumbs & Thomas, New York, 1985.

Audiovisuals for Units One and Two

Kwanzaa: A New Afro-American Holiday, a sound filmstrip by SVE, Chicago.

* "Seven Principles", a song by "Sweet Honey in the Rock" from their album, *See What the End's Gonna Be* (RR35000). Redwood Records. Also published in *Compositions: One* by Bernie Johnson Reagon, Songtalk Publishing Co., Washington, D.C., 1986.

"Jambo Means Hello", a song by Ella Jenkins, from her album *Jambo and Other Call and Response Songs and Chants.*

"Take My Hand, Precious Lord", a song by Thomas A. Dorsey, recorded in albums by various artists and printed in many hymnals.

* "Grandma's Hands", recording by Bill Withers, *Bill Withers Live at Carnegie Hall,* (SXBS-7025) and *Just As I Am* (SXBS-7006)

Nguzo Saba/Seven Principles, seven folktales animated and presented in VHS (video) format. Titles include:

"Umoja: Tiger and the Big Wind" (8 min.)

"Kujichagulia" (5 min.)

"Ujima: Modupe and the Flood" (5 min.)

"Ujamaa: Noel's Lemonade Stand" (9 min.)

"Nia" (5 min.)

"Kuumba: Simon's New Sound" (8 min.)

"Imani: Beegie and the Egg" (8 min.)

All from Beacon Films, Inc., Evanston, Illinois.

* *Say Amen, Somebody,* VHS (video) format, Pacific Arts Video and Records.

* *Author's favorites*

Free and Cued Retelling

Title: Have a Happy...

Instructions: Given orally and in writing

Free Retelling	Story Cues (examples)	Cued Retelling
	• Chris saw Jamal's bicycle near Miles's house	
	• Chris was born on Christmas Day, which Jamal said was "uncool"	
	• Chris knew he should have picked up Beth	
	•	
	•	
	•	
	•	
	•	
	•	
	•	
	•	
	•	
	•	

BESE SAKA
(Bunch of cola nuts)
Symbol of Affluence, Power,
Plenty and Togetherness.

Karamu Planning Outline

1. A karamu is_____
_____
_____
_____

2. List the things we will need for the karamu.

   _____   _____

   _____   _____

   _____   _____

   _____   _____

3. List the steps we will need to carry out in order to have the karamu.

   _____   _____

   _____   _____

   _____   _____

   _____   _____

4. Other things to consider.
_____
_____

5. Program (performance) ideas, procedures.
_____
_____
_____
_____
_____

HOW TO PRACTICE NGUZO SABA

ENRICHMENT - "HOW TO PRACTICE" NGUZO SABA
Below are slightly edited expressions of Rochester children in grades one through five. The statements were distilled from thank you letters, experience charts and other items teachers have fed back to the author.

UMOJA (oo-MOE-jah) UNITY
We can work together and play together. We must work with the people in our family and in our school and in the community of African American people.

KUJICHAGULIA (koo-jee-cha-goo-LEE-ah)
SELF-DETERMINATION
It seems hard to say, but I try and try to learn it, and learn that it's about making up my mind to "keep on keeping on" in everything I do.

UJIMA (oo-JEE-mah) COLLECTIVE WORK AND
RESPONSIBILITY
Shared work is team work. You help me and I help you...If you have a problem, you can lean on me...When I have a problem you are able to help me.

UJAMAA (oo-JAH-mah) COOPERATIVE ECONOMICS
One person alone may not have a lot; but when each person puts in her share of work, wealth and will-power, everybody has more.

NIA (nee-AH) PURPOSE
I want a good home and a good school and a good community. I will make a plan every day so I will know what to do to make the good things happen.

KUUMBA (koo-OOM-bah) CREATIVITY
I create plans for a good home and a good school and a good community...I can create beautiful things, and I will, because inside I am a beautiful person.

IMANI (ee-MAH-nee) FAITH
I believe that sharing together is good. I believe that making up my own mind and sticking to it is good too...I believe that planning and doing the right thing is good. All these things help make me beautiful inside. I believe they will help me see the beautiful old people and the little babies that will come in the future.

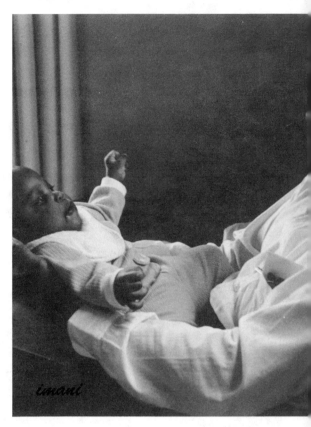

imani

NGUZO SABA

kuumba

nia

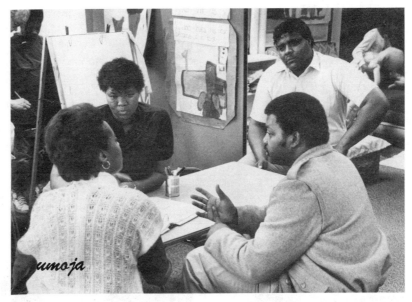

umoja

SEVEN PRINCIPLES

nujichagulia

ujima

ujamaa

AGYINDAWURU
Symbol of Alertness and Dutifulness.

58

Index

ESE NE TEKREMAH
Symbol of Improvement, Growth and Interdependence.
Prov.: "Wonnwo ba ne se" (No child is born with teeth).

AFRICAN AMERICAN HOLIDAY OF
KWANZAA (Karenga), 34
Alpha Kappa Alpha Sorority, 1,2
Angelou, Maya 38-40
    Autobiography to illustrate values
    inherent in Kwanzaa, 38-40
Anderson, Ruth, 2, 40
ASHANTI TO ZULU (Musgrove)
    practicing one's culture, 27
    relating to diversity in Atlantic Slave Trade
    27, 32
    relating to THE BLACK SNOWMAN
        (Mendez), 31
    weaving Kente cloth, special emphasis on,
    31

THE BLACK SNOWMAN (Mendez)
    cloth invested with value, 20, 21
    firefighter as resource person, 20
    kente cloth as symbol of tradition (see
        ASHANTI TO ZULU and HUGGY
        BEAN AND THE MAGIC KENTE
        CLOTH, 19
    related to fourth principle, Ujamaa, 20

Cooperative learning, 16, 33

Evaluation project 42
    report letter to relative, 42
    sample report letter, 43

Family
    extended family created by the class, 20-23
    fasting before Karamu, 8
    overarching concern, 12
    representation in HAVE A HAPPY...
        (Walter), 31,32
    representation in THE HUNDRED
        PENNY BOX (Mathis), 22-24
    representation in THE PATCHWORK
        QUILT (Flourney), 21, 22
    separations in historical context, 32
    students identifying relatives as exercise
        in Ujamaa,32, 33

Gathering in, 13
Grandma's Hands, song by Bill Withers, 21
Greetings and responses
    Habari gani (What's the news), 33
    Hujambo watoto (good morning,
        children), 17
    Kwanza yenu we na heri (Happy
        Kwanzaa), 33

Harambee (Let's all pull together), method
    of expressing, 31, 33
Harvest concept, 27
HAVE A HAPPY...(Walter) novel at the
    center of Karamu planning process, 8, 32,
    33
    family members, 29
    students read orally, 29, 30, 31, 32, 33
    Ujima, illustration of, 30
    use of story characters to enhance
        students' view of own families, 29, 30,
        31, 32
Holiday
    commemoration rather than time off, 28
    religious, ethnic, 28
HUGGY BEAN AND THE ORIGIN,
    OF THE MAGIC KENTE CLOTH (Cousins),
    20
HUNDRED PENNY BOX (Mathis)
    Habari Gani (What's the News) Journal
        student publication, 24
    illustration of Kujichagulia, 22-24
    parents relate events in children's lives
        to dates on pennies children collect, 23,
        24
    pennies in a timeline, 23, 24
    value of pennies, 23, 24

JAMBO MEANS HELLO (Feelings), 17, 29
JAMBO MEANS HELLO (Jenkins), song, 17
Johnson, James Weldon, 5, 39

Karamu
    criteria for who is to be invited, 34
    decision making process, 12, 13
    program format, 12
    implementing, 41-43
    preparation for, 33-37
Kiswahili language
    counting exercises, 19, 20
    greeting students in, 17
    JAMBO MEANS HELLO, Ella Jenkins
        song, recorded 17
    JAMBO MEANS HELLO (Feelings),
        introducing through, 17
    MOJA MEANS ONE (Feelings),
        introducing through,
        vowel sounds compared, 17
Kwanzaa
    affirmation, process and curriculum, 5
    applications to various instructional
        subjects, 11
    as all-school assembly, 27, 35
    community interprets, 6, 7

holiday, concept of, 12
how to celebrate, 7
not a substitute for, or in imitation of, 6
preparation and implementation, 7
set aside time to study, note to parents on, 21
KWANZAA (Chocolate)
relationships between child in cover illustration and people in illustration of village scene, 13
student's experiences compared to those of story character, 14
KWANZAA: A NEW AFRO-AMERICAN HOLIDAY (filmstrip), 14

MOJA MEANS ONE (Feelings),
counting exercises, 17
used to introduce Kiswahili language, 17
More Words (author's afterword), 45, 47

Nguzo Saba (Seven Principles)
children's expressions of, 15, 16
cooperative learning groups, 16, 33
definitions in the activity book, LET'S CELEBRATE KWANZAA (Thompson), 15
expressed as rap or a chant, 17, 18
posters, student made, 16, 17
resource person to introduce, 14, 15

O Black and Unknown Bards (Johnson), 38

Parents,
child's major life events, 23, 24
Karamu, invitations to, 33, 34
PATCHWORK QUILT, THE (Flourney), 21, 22
pennies, relating to child's life events, 23
Perinton (NY) African American Heritage Committee, 1, 2
PATCHWORK QUILT, THE (Flourney),
as illustration of Kuumba, 21, 22

Quilts
creating extended families out of quilt pieces, 22
memories embodied in, 21
parents as presentors on the value of, 21
physical details of, 21
profiles of those who wore the clothes from which quilt pieces came, 21
relation to multiculturalism, 22

factors involved in maintaining contact, 32, 33
locating where relatives live using maps, 32, 33
report letter to, 28, 42
Resource persons
feedback after presentation, 12
protocols, 14
Rochester Kwanzaa Committee, 1, 2
Role Play, HAVE A HAPPY...33, 34

Storytellers, value of, 11, 14
Student-led assembly as tune-up for Karamu, 34-38
call and response chant, 35, 36
enactment of HAVE A HAPPY..., Chapter 8, 33, 37, 38
props, involvement of art teacher, 37
students interpret NGUZO Saba 40, 41
Students, Frederick Douglass Middle School
Anderson, Ruth, and Sundberg, Nancy, teachers, applying Nguzo Saba, statements, 40, 41
your students, 40
Symbols, 7, 8
pronunciation of, 7, 30

Take My Hand, Precious Lord (Dorsey)
kind of person that composed it, 23
lyrics, application to, 23, 24
theme for documentary film, SAY AMEN, SOMEBODY, 24

MAP OF AFRICA

TUNISIA

MOROCCO

ALGERIA

LIBYA

EGYPT

WESTERN
SAHARA

MAURITANIA

MALI

NIGER

CHAD

SUDAN

SENEGAL

THE GAMBIA

GUINEA BISSAU

GUINEA

BURKINA

NIGERIA

ETHIOPIA

SIERRA LEONE

IVORY
COAST

BENIN
TOGO

CENTRAL AFRICAN
REPUBLIC

SOMALIA

LIBERIA

GHANA

CAMEROUN

UGANDA

KENYA

GABON

CONGO

RWANDA

ZAIRE

BURUNDI

TANZANIA

Indian Ocean

South Atlantic Ocean

ANGOLA

ZAMBIA

MALAWI

MOZAMBIQUE

ZIMBABWE

MADAGASCAR

BOTSWANA

NAMIBIA

SWAZILAND

LESOTHO

SOUTH
AFRICA

Indian Ocean

NOTES